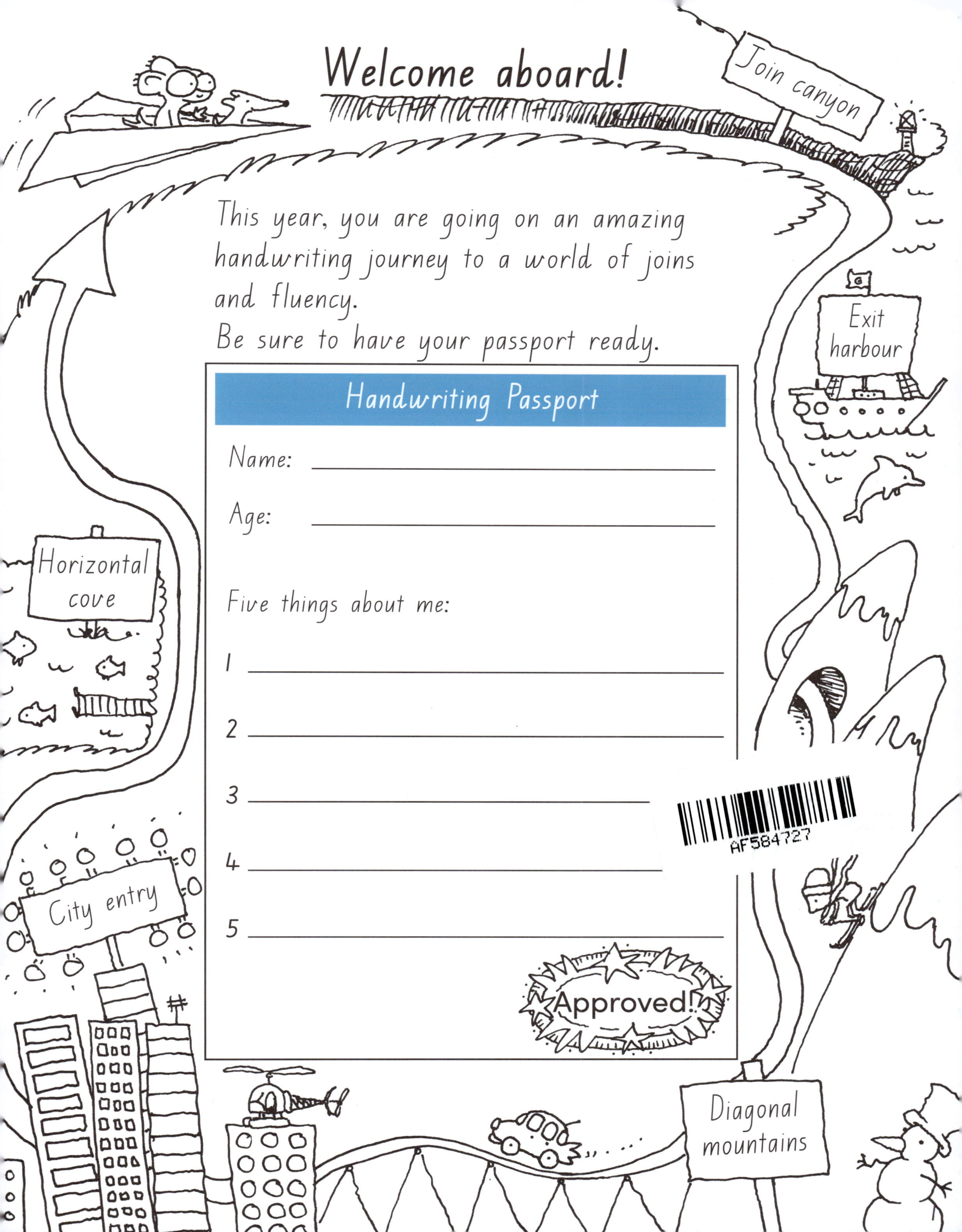

Welcome aboard!

This year, you are going on an amazing handwriting journey to a world of joins and fluency.
Be sure to have your passport ready.

Handwriting Passport

Name: ______________________

Age: ______________________

Five things about me:

1 ______________________

2 ______________________

3 ______________________

4 ______________________

5 ______________________

Review: Clockwise letters

Trace then copy.

Think about where you will start each letter.

START

Trace then write the clockwise letters.

n

m

k

p

r

h

b

j

Make up your own patterns using these letter shapes.

Handwriting: clockwise fluency patterns; Beginner's Alphabet; lower-case clockwise letter revision.

Trace then copy.

Remember to keep the slope the same.

Trace then write the straight-line letters.

l

i

z

t

x

Trace then write the direction change letters.

y

g

s

Make up your own patterns using these letter shapes.

Handwriting: downstroke fluency patterns; Beginner's Alphabet; lower-case straight-line letter revision; direction change letter revision.

Review: Anticlockwise letters

Trace then copy.

eeeeee

uuuuu

6 6 6

888888

88888888

Remember to sit the letters on the blue line correctly.

Trace then write the anticlockwise letters.

u

w

g

f

e

a

c

v

y

o

d

Handwriting: anticlockwise fluency patterns; Beginner's Alphabet; lower-case anticlockwise letter revision.

Make the letters stretch and shrink.

Handwriting: forming letters correctly; keeping slope consistent. **Literary elements:** reference to characters from *Alice's Adventures in Wonderland* by Lewis Carroll (1865).

Review: Labelling diagrams

Use these words to label the robot. Use printing to label diagrams.

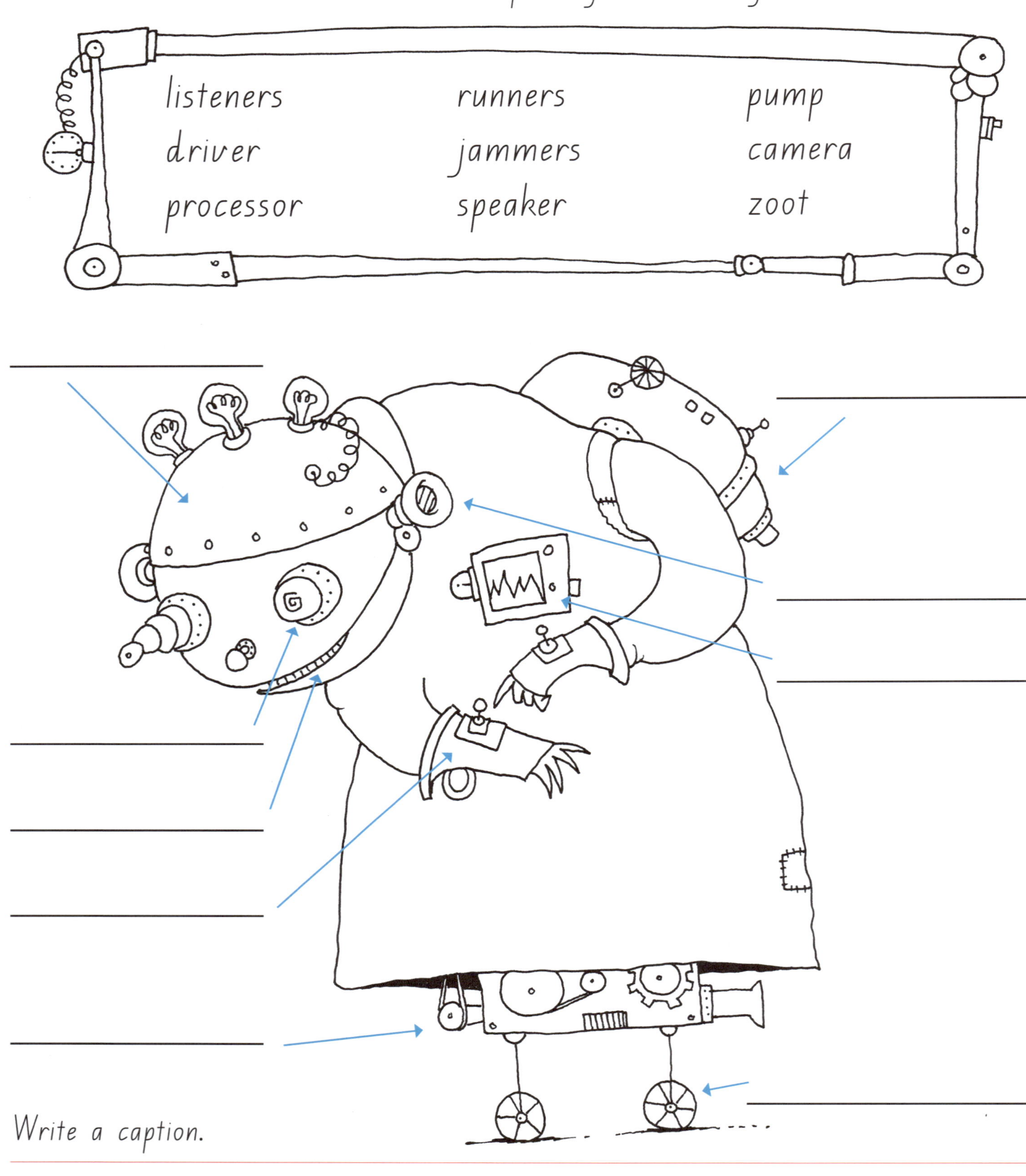

Write a caption.

Handwriting: Beginner's Alphabet; using printing to label diagrams. **Spelling and vocabulary:** technical words.
Literary elements: science fiction genre.

Capital letters are always head and body letters. Capital letters slope consistently with lower-case letters in a word.

Trace then write.

A B C D E F G H I J K L M

N O P Q R S T U V W X Y Z

Trace then write the matching capital letters.

a b c d e f g

h i j k l m n

o p q r s t u

v w x y z

Write some names of people you know. Remember to use capital letters to start.

Draw a star around your best capital letter. Draw a square around any capital letter you could improve.

Handwriting: Beginner's Alphabet and upper-case (capital) letter revision.

Trace the NATO alphabet.

Alpha Bravo
Charlie Delta
Echo Foxtrot
Golf Hotel
India Juliet
Kilo Lima
Mike November
Oscar Papa
Quebec Romeo
Sierra Tango
Uniform Victor
Whiskey X-ray
Yankee Zulu

Spell your name in the NATO alphabet.

Self assessment

My capitals are parallel to my lower-case letters:
sometimes ☐ often ☐ always ☐.

Handwriting: Beginner's Alphabet and upper-case (capital) letter revision. **Spelling and vocabulary:** alphabetical order; codes; NATO alphabet.

Trace the capital letter and then make up your own alphabet.

A B

C D

E F

G H

I J

K L

M N

O P

Q R

S T

U V

W X

Y Z

Spell a friend's name in your new alphabet.

Handwriting: Beginner's Alphabet and upper-case (capital) letter revision. **Spelling:** alphabetical order; codes.

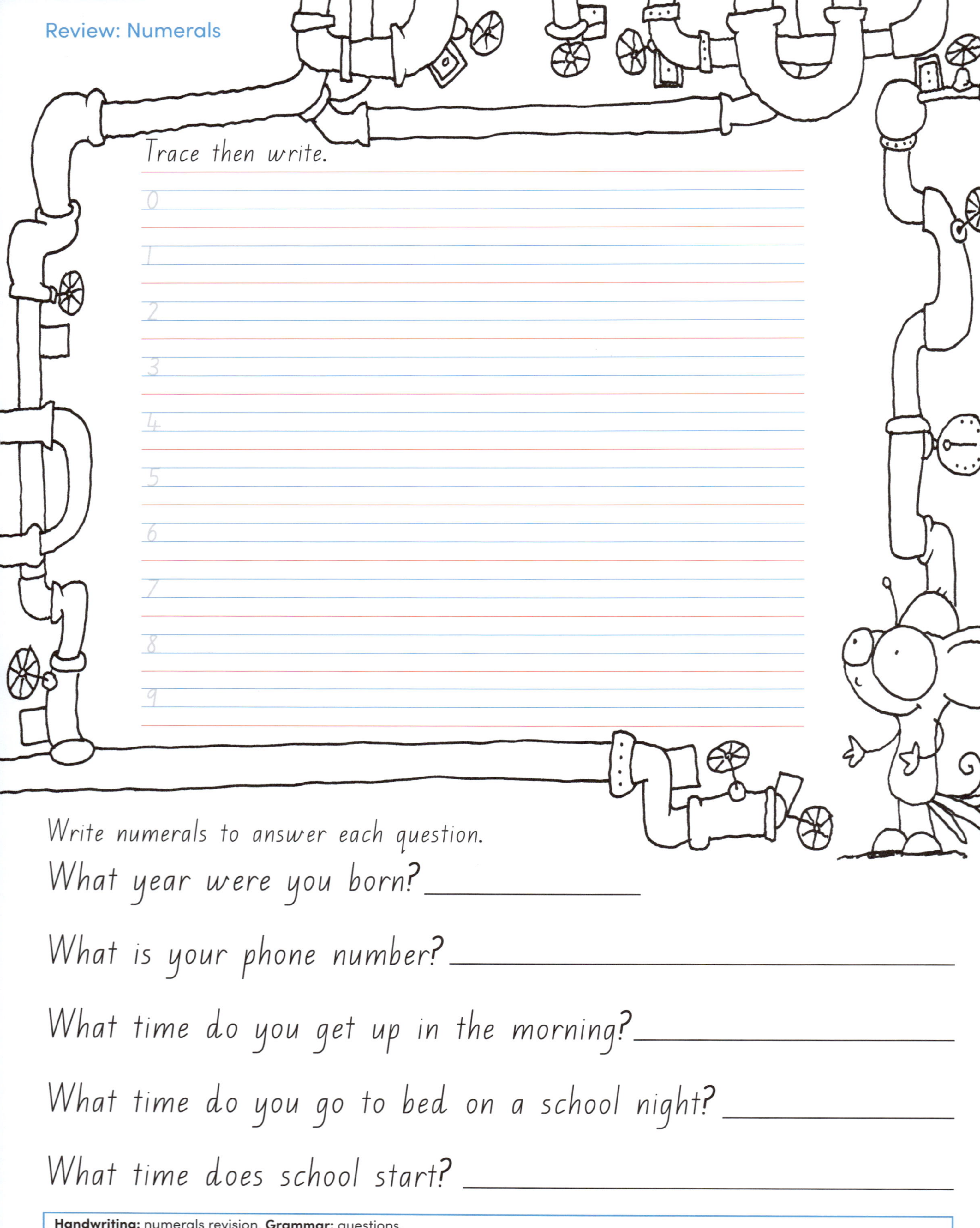

Trace then write.

0

1

2

3

4

5

6

7

8

9

Write numerals to answer each question.

What year were you born? ____________

What is your phone number? ____________

What time do you get up in the morning? ____________

What time do you go to bed on a school night? ____________

What time does school start? ____________

Handwriting: numerals revision. **Grammar:** questions.

Trace then write.

. .   , ,

' '   ' '

: :   ; ;

? ?   ! !

- -   – –

“ ”   “ ”

‘ ’

Trace then write.

“What do you call a collection of letters?”

asked the teacher.

“That’s the alphabet!” shouted the class.

Handwriting: Beginner’s Alphabet and punctuation revision. **Grammar:** collective noun (class); saying verbs (asked, shouted); being verbs (‘is’ in That’s). **Punctuation:** full stop; comma; question mark; exclamation mark; colon; semi-colon; hyphen; dash; apostrophe; quotation marks. **Spelling and vocabulary:** apostrophe for contraction (That’s).

Watch your letter size, letter shape and slope. Make sure your letters face the right way.

Rewrite the text correctly.

“WHat dO You CALL a grOUP of chilDren?”

asked Sanjay.

“That's a ɔlass!” yellEd RoSie.

“You're corrEcT”, saidthetEAcHer.

Self assessment

My letter shapes: need to improve ☐ are good ☐ are fantastic ☐.

My letter sizes: are inconsistent ☐ are good ☐ are fantastic ☐.

My letter slope: is inconsistent ☐ is good ☐ is consistently good ☐.

Handwriting: slope; letter shape; letter size. **Grammar:** question; exclamation; saying verbs (asked, yelled); collective noun (class); proper nouns (Rosie, Sanjay); being verbs ('is' in That's, 'are' in You're). **Punctuation**: full stop; upper-case (capital) letter to start a sentence; exclamation mark; question mark; quotation marks. **Spelling and vocabulary**: apostrophe for contraction (That's, You're).

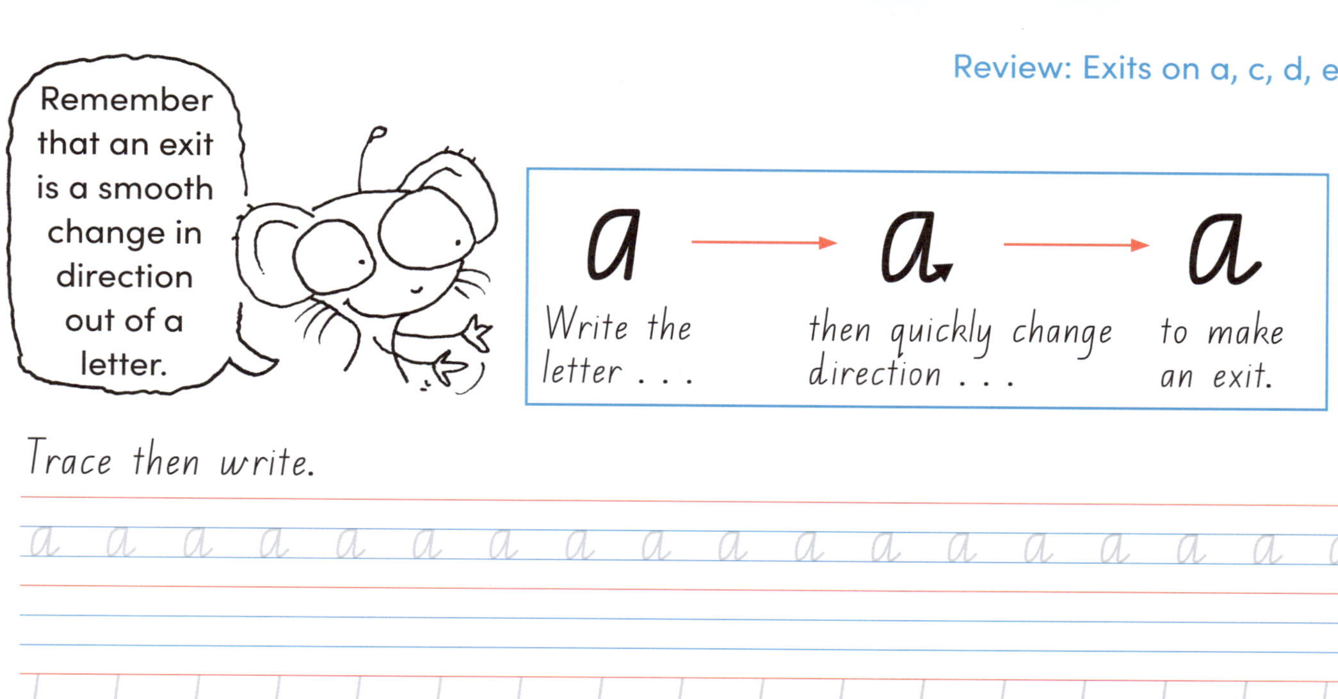

Trace then write.

a a a a a a a a a a a a a a a a a a a

h h h h h h h h h h h h h h h h h h

k k k k k k k k k k k k k k k k k

l l l l l l l l l l l l l l l l l l l l l l l

t t t t t t t t t t t t t t t

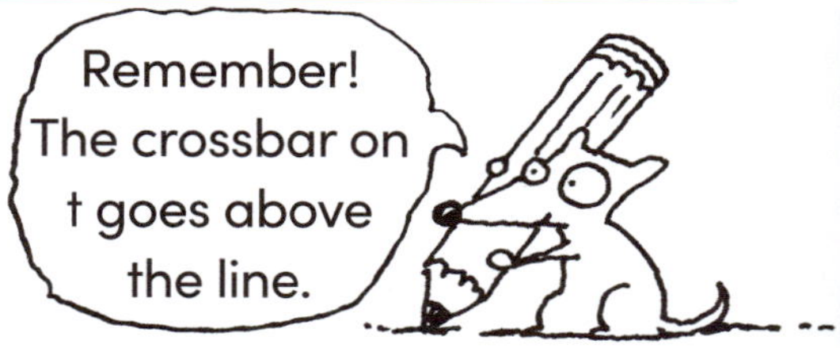

Remember! The crossbar on t goes above the line.

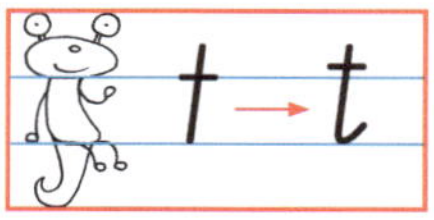

t → t

c c c c c c c c c c c c c c

e e e e e e e e e e e e e e e e e e e e e

d d d d d d d d d d d d d d d d d d

Handwriting: quick, smooth exits from a, c, d, e, h, k, l, t.

Trace then write.

r r r r r r r r r r r r r r r r r r r r

m m m m m m m m m m m m m m m

n n n n n n n n n n n n n n n n n n

x x x x x x x x x x x x x x x x x x x

x x x x x x x x x x x x x x x x x x x

Trace then write.

mix wax box axe relax index text

Handwriting: letters with rounded entries r, m, n, x.

Handwriting: letters with pointed entries i, j, p, u, v, w, y. **Spelling and vocabulary:** rhyme (beans/jeans). **Literary elements:** spoonerisms.

Review: Letters that change – f

Trace then write.

f f f f f f f f f f f f f f f f

gulf leaf deaf gift sift lift

life wife strife fluff stuff

In the sea, once upon a time . . .

there was a Whale, and he ate fishes.

He ate the starfish and the garfish . . .

and the really truly twirly-whirly eel.

Self assessment

My f's are a good shape:

sometimes ☐ often ☐ always ☐.

Handwriting: new shape for the letter f. **Grammar:** noun group for eel has an article, adverbs and an adjective. **Punctuation**: ellipses to indicate words have been left out (. . .). **Spelling and vocabulary**: rhyme (gift/lift, life/strife, twirly-whirly). **Literary elements**: quote from *Just So Stories*, 'How the Whale Got His Throat', by Rudyard Kipling (1902); common story beginning phrase 'once upon a time.'

Remember! z has changed shape to make it easier to join to z.

Start with a rounded entry and go down . . . then branch up a little . . . make a quick turn and drop down. Finish along the line.

Trace then write.

z z z z z z z z z z z z z z z z z z z z

Trace then write.

"Here is the repulsant snozzcumber!"

cried the BFG, waving it about.

"I squoggle it! I mispise it! I dispunge it!"

Make up some words of your own.

Handwriting: new shape for letter z. **Grammar:** statement; exclamation; adjective (repulsant); saying verb (cried); doing verb (waving); thinking verbs (squoggle, mispise, dispunge); noun (snozzcumber); noun-pronoun reference chain (snozzcumber/it); acronym (BFG). **Punctuation**: full stop; upper-case (capital) letter to start a sentence; exclamation mark; comma; quotation marks. **Spelling and vocabulary**: negative prefixes mis- (in mispise for despise), dis- (in dispunge meaning to expunge or erase). **Literary elements**: quote from *The BFG* by Roald Dahl (1982); neologism (snozzcumber); portmanteau word (repulsant = repulsive and unpleasant).

Diagonal joins to rounded entries

a →	a →	an
Make an exit . . .	then keep going up . . .	until you get to the rounded entry.

Use a diagonal join . . .

from any of these letters	to any of these rounded entries.
a c d e h i k l m n t u x	m n r x z

Trace then write the letter pairs. Remember to use diagonal joins.

am an ar ax az dr er am an ar ax az

em en ex ez im in ir em en ex ez im

km mm iz uz nn tr cr km mm iz uz

fizz fuzz pizza winning pink trinket

swimmer crime drink think ink crank

Handwriting: diagonal joins to rounded entries. **Grammar**: question; personal pronoun (you); noun group (your paw). **Punctuation**: question mark. **Spelling and vocabulary**: homophones (pour/paw).

Trace then write.

man pan arm axe maze dry laundry

germ gem pen exit breeze sneeze den

trim tin girl knee swimming running

Trace then write. Remember to use diagonal joins.

loan lone

main mane

pain pane

pair pear

paw pour

rain rein

raw roar

hear here

Can you pour with your paw?

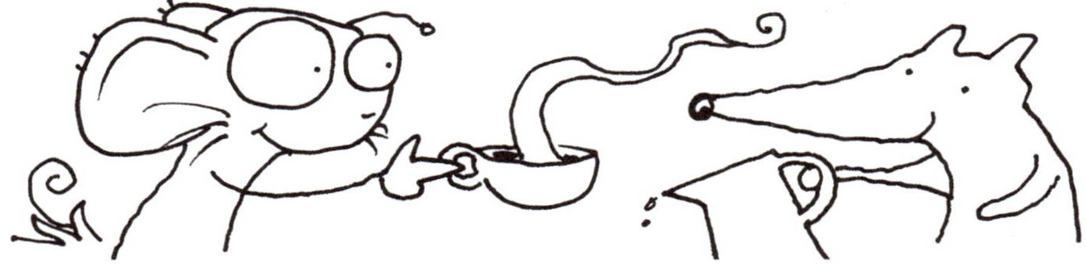

Use a diagonal join...

from any of these letters	to any of these pointed entries.
a c d e h i k l m n t u x	i j p u v w y

Trace then write.

ai aj ap au av aw ay iy ap au av aw

ip iv iw ij di du dw hi ip iv iw ij di

hu li lu ki ku mi mu hu li lu ki ku

ni nu ap xi xu ui ti tu ni nu ap xi xu

pip pup puppy jump hump lump hip lip

pump mumps primp live hive dwindle

Handwriting: diagonal joins to pointed entries.

Trace then write.

paid ajar ape caught aim eject enjoy

paw pay drip dirt dirty few drew hum

dug him mum nip nut dip supper

apple fruit time tired pixie tiny tin

ay day pay say may hay ray play stay

aw paw draw drawer raw gnaw straw

ai rain drain brain pain raincoat plain

av pave rave gave slave grave shave

My diagonal joins are smooth:
sometimes ☐ often ☐ always ☐.

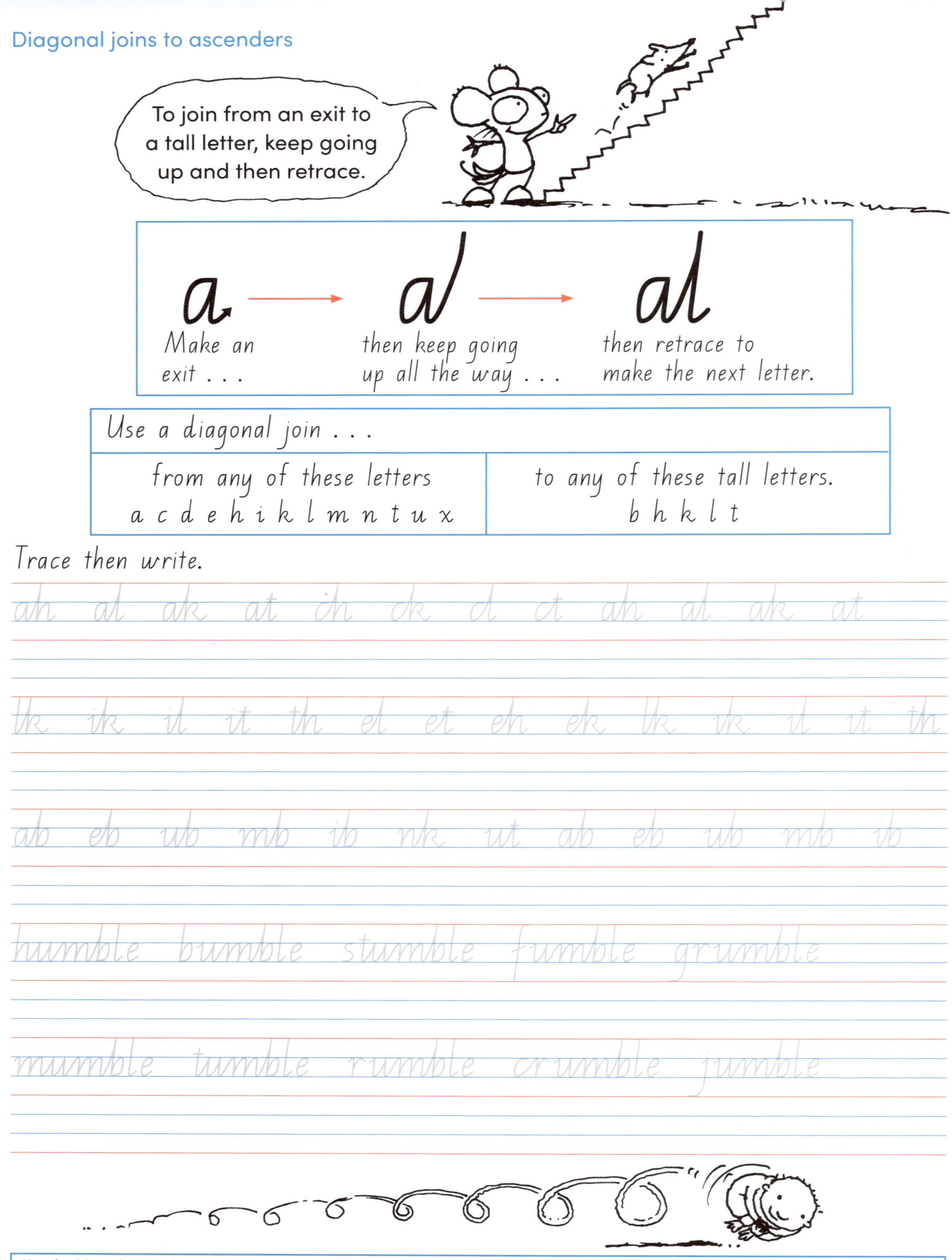

Use a diagonal join . . .	
from any of these letters a c d e h i k l m n t u x	to any of these tall letters. b h k l t

Trace then write.

ah al ak at ch ck cl ct ah al ak at

lk ik il it th el et eh ek lk ik il it th

ab eb ub mb ib nk ut ab eb ub mb ib

humble bumble stumble fumble grumble

mumble tumble rumble crumble jumble

Handwriting: diagonal joins to ascenders b, h, k, l, t. **Spelling and vocabulary**: rhyme (humble/bumble); words ending in 'le'.

Trace then write.

hill till mill

ant lent bent rent sent spent went

pet met milk hut hunt mud shut haunt

tilt hilt kilt lilt with pith path fault

mint lint tint hint dint hat splat sprint

walk talk chalk will kill pill chill grill

wet sheet tweet web dab grab habit rabbit

Rate your diagonal joins on a scale from 1 to 5. 1 means you need a lot more practice. 5 means your joins are fantastic.

1 2 3 4 5

Handwriting: diagonal joins to ascenders b, h, k, l, t. **Spelling:** common letter pairs.

Diagonal joins to o

Take the exit up to the blue line. Then retrace the top a little.

Use a diagonal join to o . . . from any of these letters.
a c d e h i k l m n t u x

Trace then write.

co co coat do do dog ho ho hot

lo lo log mo mo mop no no not

to to top co co colt mo mo moan

It's raining cats and dogs.

Trace then write. Put a tick under the diagonal joins.

Fern loved Wilbur

more than anything.

Handwriting: diagonal joins to the letter o. **Grammar**: proper nouns (Fern, Wilbur); thinking verb (loved). **Literary elements**: idiom (raining cats and dogs); quote from *Charlotte's Web* by EB White (1952).

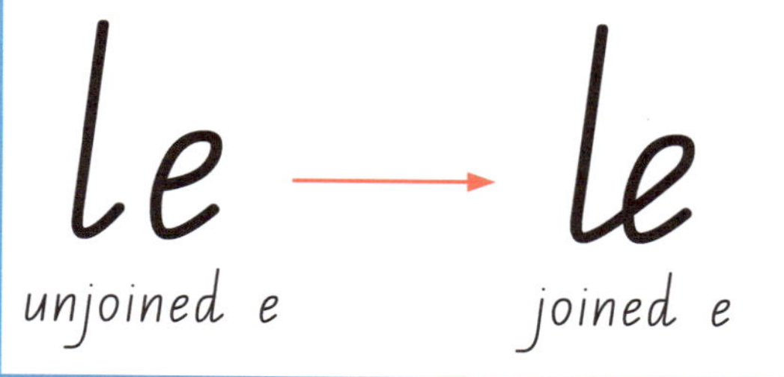

Use a diagonal join to e . . .
from any of these letters.
a c d e h i k l m n t u x

Trace then write.

ce de ee ee he ie ke ce de ee ee he ie

le me ne te ue xe xe le me ne te ue xe

ce piece de deep de den he heel ie belief

ie chief ke keep ke kelp le leap me meal

ne need te team te athlete ue duel xe axe

The early bird catches the worm.

Handwriting: diagonal joins to e. **Spelling and vocabulary**: vowel digraphs 'ee', 'ie', 'ea'.

Practise more diagonal joins.

Trace then write the homophones.

cue queue

days daze

blew blue

quay key

knew new

tail tale

eight ate

maize maze

flower flour

Write a sentence of your own using one or more of the word pairs. Remember to use diagonal joins.

Self assessment

My diagonal joins are smooth: sometimes ☐ often ☐ always ☐.

I retraced neatly: sometimes ☐ often ☐ always ☐.

Handwriting: diagonal joins revision. **Spelling and vocabulary:** homophones.

Trace then write the letter pairs. Remember to use diagonal joins.

eb th tt tl dt dl eb th tt tl dt dl

ht hl kl kh ll lt ht hl kl kh ll lt

Trace then write. Use diagonal joins where you need to.

knight night

knit nit

cent sent scent

wait weight

sail sale

meat meet

Did you see the nit knit?

Is this blue sail on sale?

The knight fought the dragon through the night.

weather whether

My diagonal joins are smooth:
sometimes ☐ often ☐ always ☐.

Handwriting: diagonal joins revision. **Grammar:** past tense doing verb (fought); prepositional phase (through the night).
Punctuation: question mark. **Spelling and vocabulary:** common letter pairs/groups 'ee', 'ai,' 'ght'; homophones.

a	→	a	→	pencil lift ac
Make an exit . . .		then keep going up . . .		lift your pencil and drop on the letter.

Use exits from any of these letters	to drop on any of these letters.
a c d e h i k l m n t u x	a c d g q

Trace then write.

ac ad ag aq ca cc cd ac ad ag aq ca cc cd ac ad

da dg ea ec ed eg eq da dg ea ec ed eg eq da dg

ha ia ic id ig iq ka ha ia ic id ig iq ka ha ia ic

la ld ac ad ag ca da la ld ac ad ag ca da la ld ac

id ld la iq ta ng ug xa id ld la iq ta ng ug xa id

Make sure that the back of the dropped on letter touches the long exit.

Handwriting: dropping on letters a, c, d, g, q. **Grammar**: request; quoted speech. **Punctuation**: quotation marks; exclamation mark.
Spelling and vocabulary: common final consonant blends (ld, nd); rhyme (fudge/grudge); u always follows q; homophones (racket/racquet).

Trace then write.

sing thing ring ding string spring thing

stand band land hand brand grand sand

hold gold bold sold fold told cold mold

judge fudge grudge nudge budge trudge

Trace then write.

"Please quit making a racket with that racquet!"

said the quoll.

Make sure that the back of the dropped on letter touches the long exit.

Trace. Then write five words for each letter pair. The first one has been done for you.

ud mud thud cloud proud loud

da

ha

id

ld

ta

ug

ag

Drop a letter a, c, d, g or q on to each word. Then write the word.

m ny	u ly	bla k
di	fud e	slud e
li uid	t ke	l ter
m ke	m le	mu dy
sow	ban	du k
bou uet		

Handwriting: dropping on letters a, c, d, g, q. **Spelling and vocabulary**: rhyme (trail/snail). **Literary elements**: proverb; idiom; spoonerisms.

Trace then write.

Many hands make light work.

Practice makes perfect.

Trace then write the spoonerisms.

TRAIL SNACKS

trail snacks – snail tracks

eye ball – bye all

picking your nose –

nicking your pose

Find or make up a spoonerism of your own. Write it here.

Self assessment

I feel confident about dropping on letters:

sometimes ☐ mostly ☐ always ☐.

Handwriting: horizontal joins to rounded entries; consistency of size. **Spelling**: common letter pairs.

Trace then write.

rr purr furry hurry wn town gown

rm worm form storm warm charm

on only or short story

oz dozen oz woozy on lonely

wr wrap wrong wring ox toxic

Copy the words and make them stretch. Be careful with the horizontal joins.

arm

only

toxic

lonely

Horizontal joins to pointed entries

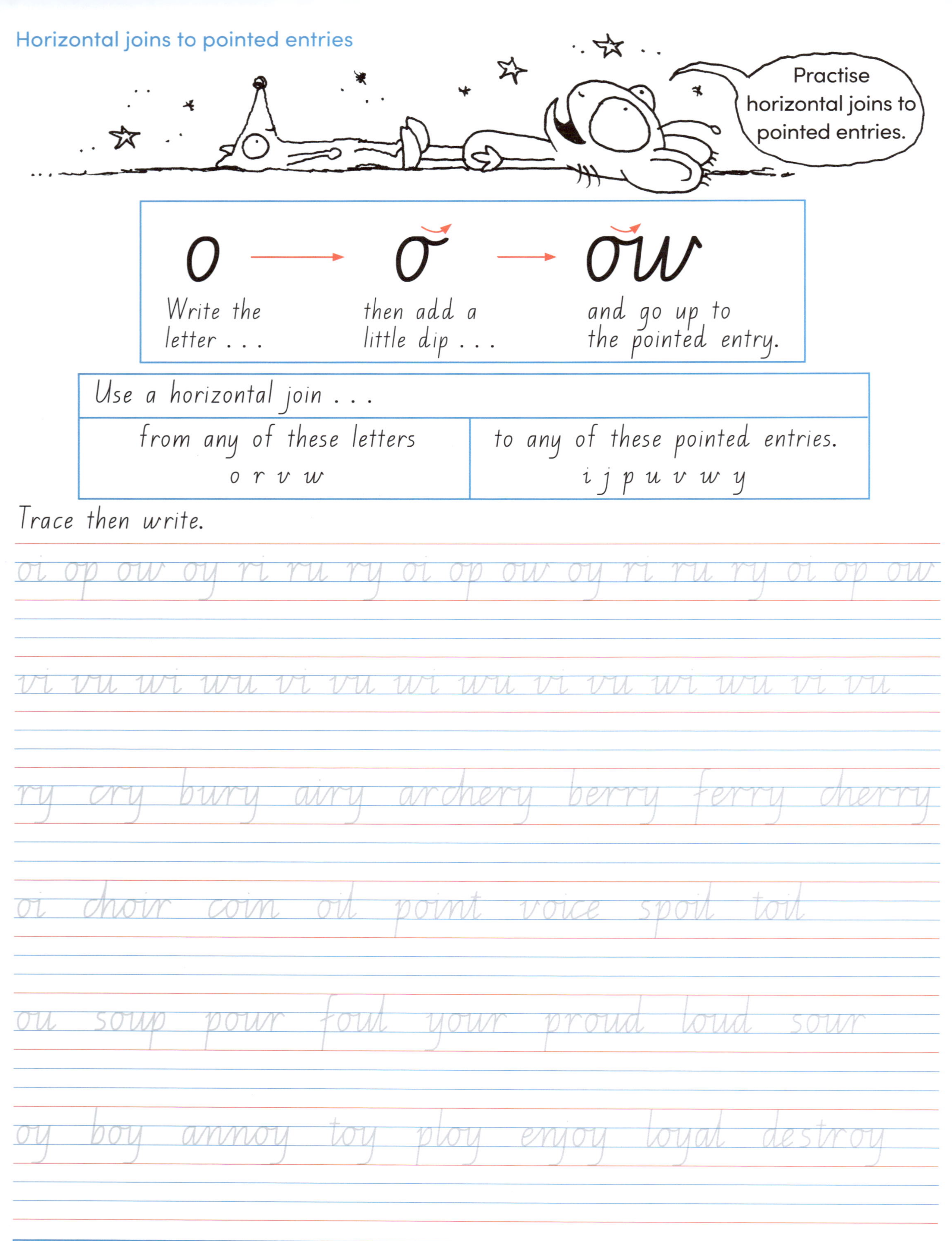

o → o → ow

Write the letter . . . then add a little dip . . . and go up to the pointed entry.

Use a horizontal join . . .	
from any of these letters o r v w	to any of these pointed entries. i j p u v w y

Trace then write.

oi op ow oy ri ru ry oi op ow oy ri ru ry oi op ow

vi vu wi wu vi vu wi wu vi vu wi wu vi vu

ry cry bury airy archery berry ferry cherry

oi choir coin oil point voice spoil toil

ou soup pour foul your proud loud sour

oy boy annoy toy ploy enjoy loyal destroy

Handwriting: horizontal joins to pointed entries. **Spelling and vocabulary**: digraphs 'ou', 'oy', 'oi'.

Trace then write.

vi vu wi wu oi ou op oy vi vu wi wu oi ou op oy

ov ow ri ru rp wy wu wi ov ow ri ru rp wy wu

vi vine viper vital vigorous heaviness

ow tow show snow below window stow

rp burp slurp harp

SLURP

ri ripe script wrist

ru run rust runny running erupt crumb

wi wipe with win willow swift swindle

vu vulture

op open opposite

You need a horizontal join . . .	
from any of these letters o r v w	to sweep up to these tall letters. b h k l t

Trace then write.

ob oh ok ol ot ob oh ok ol ot ob oh ok ol ot ob oh

rb rk rb rk rb rk rb rk wh rl rt wh rl rt wh

rl girl curl hurl whirl twirl darling

rk work fork lurk quirk dark jerk

rt hurt sort flirt dirt splurt skirt heart

Handwriting: horizontal joins to ascenders b, h, k, l, t. **Grammar**: question; statement. **Punctuation**: quotation marks; question mark; comma; full stop. **Spelling and vocabulary**: apostrophe for contractions (didn't, who's); digraphs 'wh' and 'oo' (whoosh, whoop), 'or' (snort, chortle), 'ar' (snarl), 'ur' (hurt), 'ir' (girl); silent k (know, knock). **Literary elements**: knock knock joke; onomatopoeia.

Trace then write.

"Knock, knock." "Who's there?"

"Who." "Who who?"

"I didn't know you were an owl."

Trace then write the onomatopoeia words.

whiz whirr wham whisk

whack whoosh whoop

snarl bawl growl hoot

chortle howl snort

Hoot

Snort

Write some onomatopoeia words of your own. Tick any horizontal joins where you needed to retrace.

Self assessment

My retracing on horizontal joins is smooth:

sometimes ☐ often ☐ always ☐.

Horizontal joins to anticlockwise letters

Use a horizontal join . . .	
from any of these letters o r v w	to any of these letters. a c d g o q

Trace then write.

oa oc od og od oo oq oa oc oa oc od og od oo oq

ra rc rd rg ro rq ra rc ra rc rd rg ro rq ra rc

va vo wa wo va vo va vo wa wo va vo wa wo

dock oar crowd dog rage roast room

water vase road wage

race worm vroom vroom

Handwriting: horizontal joins to anticlockwise letters a, c, d, g, o, q. **Grammar**: statements; exclamation; thinking verb (wondered); proper nouns (Pooh, Pharaoh); collective noun (herd). **Punctuation**: full stop; exclamation mark; upper-case (capital) letter to start a sentence. **Spelling and vocabulary**: rhyme (large/charge); homophone (herd/heard); tricky words (wondered/wandered). **Literary elements**: reference to character (Winnie-the-Pooh) from *When We Were Very Young* by AA Milne (1924).

Make sure the space between letters is regular.

Trace then write. Draw a circle around rd and rg.

I heard the herd of goats.

I saw the large rhino charge.

I wondered about the racoons

as I wandered around the zoo.

Trace then write.

rock flock hood food

Pooh Pharaoh look book

Look how Pooh spells honey!

My retracing is smooth:

sometimes ☐ mostly ☐ always ☐.

Letters that don't join

Handwriting: letters that end in a clockwise direction (b, g, j, p, s, y, z) don't join to the next letter; q doesn't join to u. **Grammar**: collective nouns; articles (a/an). **Spelling and vocabulary**: rhyme (slugs/bugs); q is always followed by u; tricky words (quiet and quite).

Trace then write. If a letter ends in a clockwise direction, remember **not** to join it to the next letter.

a gaggle of geese

a band of coyotes

a tribe of goats

a shadow of jaguars

an ambush of tigers

a prickle of porcupines

Make up your own collective nouns.

a of slugs

a of bugs

a of gnats

a of bats

a of ghosts

a of pillows

a of knives

a of forks

Self assessment

Others find my handwriting easy to read:

rarely ☐ mostly ☐ always ☐.

oe re ve we

These letters don't join to e.

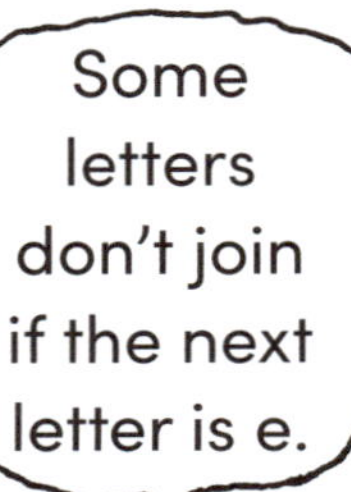

Trace then write.

a covey of quail
a drove of cattle
a shiver of sharks
a business of ferrets
a tower of giraffes
a drove of hares

Trace then write.

I have a very large, hot dog.

I have a very large hot dog.

When I write, my hand and arm are relaxed and comfortable: rarely ☐ mostly ☐ always ☐.

Handwriting: letters o, r, v, w don't join to e. **Grammar**: collective nouns. **Punctuation**: use of a comma can change meaning in a sentence.

Handwriting: joins from f. **Spelling and vocabulary**: rhyme (fum/come). **Literary elements**: reference to folktale, *Jack and the Beanstalk*.

To join **to** f you need to make a loop.

Write the letter and go up.

Then make a small loop to go down.

Lift your pencil and use the crossbar to join to the next letter.

Look! These are diagonal joins.

Trace then write.

af df ef if lf uf kf

chafe steadfast chief rift breakfast

wolf tuft elf shelf yourself calf

Look! These are horizontal joins.

proof butterfly woof scarf

often roof turf surf

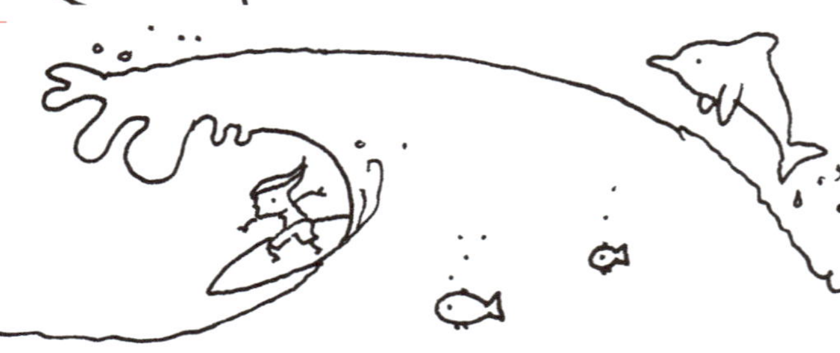

Handwriting: diagonal joins to f; horizontal joins to f; joins from f. **Spelling and vocabulary**: common letter pairs 'lf', 'rf'.

Look! f has no loop after clockwise finishing letters.

Trace then write.

tubful capful cupful playful helpful bagful

joyful boyfriend bellyful wayfarer crayfish

playful playfully playfulness

Double f has two loops!

off

Use the crossbar to loop to the second f.

Trace then write.

stiff sniff stuff puff huff scoff toffee

huffy puffy stuffy scruffy fluffy sniffly

gruff truffle wiffle waffle raffle snuffle

I am confident when joining to and from f:

sometimes ☐ often ☐ always ☐.

Handwriting: joins to and from f; letters that finish in a clockwise direction do not join to f; joining ff. **Spelling and vocabulary**: compound words (boyfriend); word families (playful, playfully); suffix (ful); rhyme (huff/puff, stuffy/scruffy).

o → o → os (retrace)

Write the letter . . . then extend the horizontal join over the top of s . . . and retrace back around.

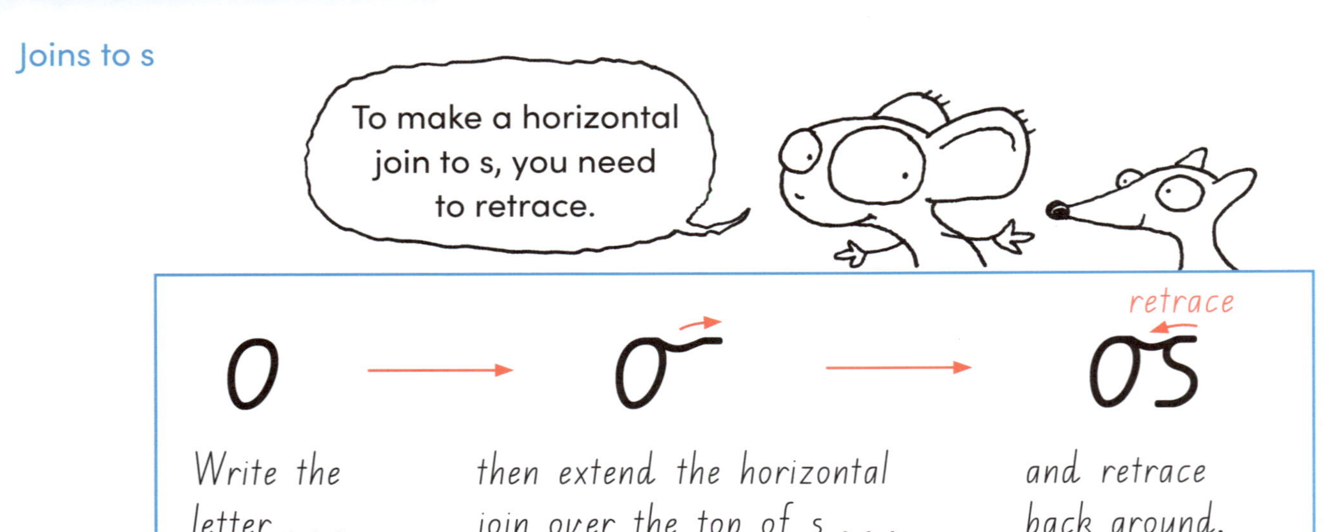

Trace then write.

os os os os os os os os os os os os os os

rs rs rs rs rs rs rs rs rs rs rs rs rs

vs vs vs vs vs vs vs vs vs vs vs vs

ws ws ws ws ws ws ws ws ws ws ws

lose lost loose loosely rose roost boost host

horse stars cars bars harsh marsh course

jaws paws grows gnaws shows drowsy cows

Handwriting: horizontal joins to s. **Spelling and vocabulary**: rhyme (jaws/paws/gnaws); silent g (gnaws).

Make a diagonal exit . . .

and keep going to just above the blue line.

Then retrace a little and finish the bottom of s.

Trace then write.

as as as as ds ds ds ds ds es es es es

is is is ks ks ks ks is is is ks ks ks

ls ls ls ls ms ms ms ms ns ns ns ns

ts ts ts ts ts ts ts us us us us us us

wish chicks girls heads casual oranges

bones swarms hens tents rust apples eyes

Handwriting: diagonal joins to s.

oss iss

It's easier if you let double ss's be twins.

Trace then write.

ss ss ss ss ss ss oss oss oss oss oss oss

ass ess iss uss ass ess iss uss ass ess

iss uss ass ess iss uss ass ess iss uss

pass dress miss fuss loss losses

brass stress hiss busses floss flosses

What a fuss!

Handwriting: joins to s; joining double s when s shape has changed. **Grammar**: adjectives (glassy, classy, bossy); exclamation; modal adverbs (possibly, impossibly); suffixes for tense (tossed, tossing). **Punctuation**: exclamation mark. **Spelling and vocabulary**: word families (boss/bosses/bossy); suffix –ly; antonyms (possible/impossible); negative prefix im– (impossible).

Trace then write.

ss ss ss ss ss ss ss ss ss ss ss ss ss ss

ass ess iss uss ass ess iss uss ass ess

oss oss oss oss oss oss oss

toss tossed tossing tosses

gloss glosses glossy boss bosses bossy

moss mosses mossy class classes classy

glass glasses glassy dress dresses dressy

possible impossible possibly impossibly

possibility impossibility impressive unimpressive

I am confident when joining to s:

sometimes ☐ often ☐ always ☐.

Join up as much of your writing as you can using all the joins you have learned.

Trace then write these sentences about book characters.

Pinocchio was made of wood.

Pippi Longstocking had red hair.

Mowgli lived in the jungle.

Veruca Salt won the second golden ticket.

Augustus Gloop loved chocolate.

Find some other book character names. Write them here in your best writing.

Self assessment

I enjoy writing with joined letters:

sometimes ☐ usually ☐ always ☐ .

Handwriting: practising all joins. **Grammar**: proper nouns upper-case (capital). **Punctuation**: upper-case (capital) letter for proper nouns; upper-case (capital) letter to start a sentence; full stop. **Literary elements**: references to characters and settings from *Pippi Longstocking* by Astrid Lindgren (1945), *The Jungle Book* by Rudyard Kipling (1894), *The Adventures of Pinocchio* by Carlo Collodi (1883), *Charlie and the Chocolate Factory* by Roald Dahl (1964), *The Road to Oz* by Frank L Baum (1909), *The Lion the Witch and the Wardrobe* by CS Lewis (1950), *Alice in Wonderland* by Lewis Carroll (1865), *Peter Pan and Wendy* by JM Barrie (1911).

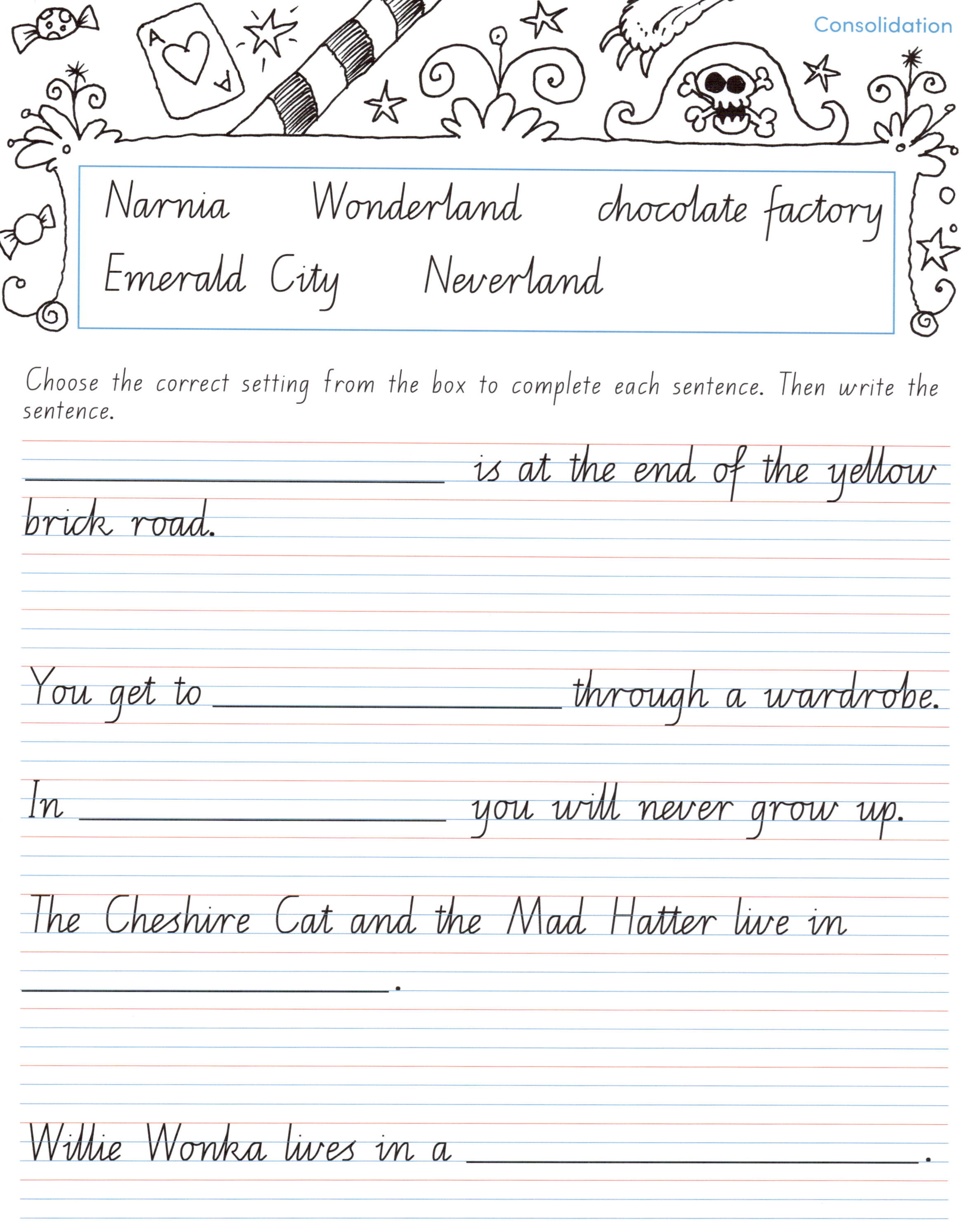

Narnia Wonderland chocolate factory
Emerald City Neverland

Choose the correct setting from the box to complete each sentence. Then write the sentence.

_______________ is at the end of the yellow brick road.

You get to _______________ through a wardrobe.

In _______________ you will never grow up.

The Cheshire Cat and the Mad Hatter live in _______________.

Willie Wonka lives in a _______________.

Trace then write.

"Why did you call him Tortoise, if he wasn't one?"

Alice asked.

"We called him Tortoise because he taught us."

said the Mock Turtle angrily.

What might Alice reply to the Mock Turtle? Write Alice's speech here. Remember to use quotation marks.

Handwriting: practising all joins. **Grammar:** adverb (angrily); reference (Tortoise-one); proper nouns (Tortoise, Mock Turtle); pronouns (you, him, he, we, us); compound sentence; conjunctions (if, because). **Punctuation**: quotation marks; question mark; comma; full stop; upper-case (capital) letter for proper nouns and to start a sentence. **Spelling and vocabulary**: apostrophe for contraction (wasn't); digraphs 'au' (because, taught), 'or' (tortoise). **Literary elements:** pun/word play (tortoise/taught us); quote from *Alice's Adventures in Wonderland* by Lewis Carroll (1865).

Trace then write the similes.

as hungry as a wolf

as wary as a fox

as loyal as a dog

as brave as a lion

as fierce as a tiger

drools like a hungry monster

surfs like a clown

as cold as ice

Handwriting: practising all joins. **Literary elements**: similes using 'like' or 'as'; reference to folk tale, *Little Red Riding Hood*.

Trace then write. Link each underlined noun group with its meaning on the right.

Look out for <u>a Noah's Ark</u>.

Have <u>a Captain Cook</u>.

What's <u>the John Dory</u>?

Let's hit <u>the frog and toad</u>.

I'll have <u>a dog's eye</u>.

Have you fed <u>the hollow log</u>?

Answer <u>the dog and bone</u>.

the dog
a look
the road
a pie
the story
a shark
the phone

Handwriting: practising all joins. **Grammar:** noun groups; proper nouns (Noah's Ark, John Dory); question; possessive apostrophes (Noah's, butcher's, dog's). **Punctuation**: question mark. **Literary elements**: rhyming slang.

This is a quote from a story called *The Tale of Peter Rabbit.*

Trace then write.

Don't go into Mr McGregor's garden:

your Father had an accident there;

he was put in a pie by Mrs McGregor.

Write a safety warning of your own. It can be a warning for a friend, family member, or story character. It can be sensible or silly.

Handwriting: practising all joins. **Grammar:** warnings (Don't); commands start with a verb or verb group (Do not go); possessive apostrophe (Mr McGregor's); proper noun (McGregor). **Punctuation**: colon; semicolon. **Spelling and vocabulary**: apostrophe for contraction (Don't). **Literary elements**: play on words and understatement (accident/put in a pie); quote from *The Tale of Peter Rabbit* by Beatrix Potter (1902).

This quote is from a story called *The Road to Oz*. Polychrome is the Rainbow's daughter.

Trace then write.

"Haven't you any dewdrops, or mist-cakes,

or cloudbuns?" asked Polychrome, longingly.

"Course not," replied Dorothy.

Dewdrops, mist-cakes and cloudbuns are food that Polychrome likes to eat. Make up some food words of your own that you think sound delicious. Draw them.

Handwriting: practising all joins. **Grammar:** question; negative question word (Haven't); adverb (longingly); saying verbs (asked, replied). **Punctuation**: quotation marks; question mark; commas to separate items in a list; full stop; upper-case (capital) letter for proper noun (Polychrome). **Spelling and vocabulary**: apostrophe for contraction (haven't); Poly meaning many; chrome from Greek 'chroma' meaning colour. **Literary elements**: quote from *The Road to Oz* by L Frank Baum (1909); play on food and weather words (dewdrops, mist-cakes, cloudbuns).

Add as many labels as you can think of to the map. Remember to use printing to label maps and diagrams.

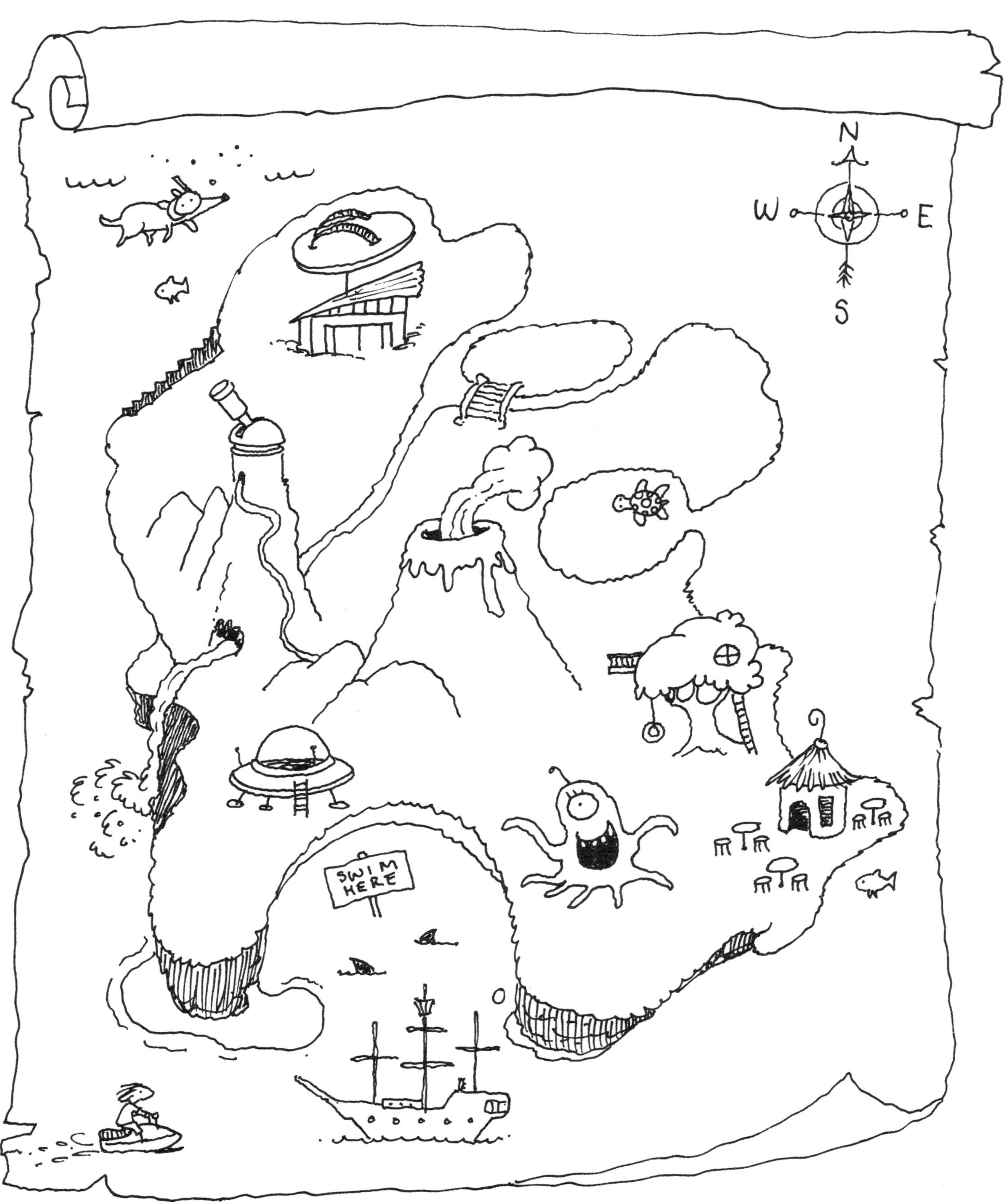

Handwriting: using printing to label maps and diagrams. **Literary elements:** fantasy.

Dr Doolittle is a story character who could talk to animals. This is a quote from him.

"Oh that," said the Doctor, turning around – "that's a Wiff-Waff. Its full name is hippocampus pippitopitus."

Scientific name: hippocampus pippitopitus

Rewrite the quote. Use all the joins you know.

Make up your own creature and give it a scientific sounding name. Draw a picture of it. Label its features.

Remember to use printing for labels.

Handwriting: practising all joins; printing for labels. **Grammar:** pronouns (that, that's, its). **Punctuation:** quotation marks; comma. **Spelling and vocabulary**: made-up words. **Literary elements**: quote from *The Voyages of Doctor Doolittle* by Hugo Lofting (1922).

Trace the nonsense poem.

JABBERWOCKY by Lewis Carroll

'Twas brillig, and the slithy toves
Did gyre and gimble in the wabe:
All mimsy were the borogoves,
And the mome raths outgrabe.

Here are some more nonsense words. Write a meaning for each one. Then complete the table with some more nonsense words of your own.

NONSENSE WORD	PART OF SPEECH	MEANING
snismy	adjective	
groot	verb	
borotroves	noun	

Handwriting: upper-case (capital) letters; cursive. **Grammar:** parts of speech. **Punctuation:** apostrophe; comma; colon.
Spelling and vocabulary: nonsense words; portmanteau words (slithy = lithe and slimy, mimsy = miserable and flimsy).
Literary elements: poetry (ballad); quote from 'Jabberwocky' from *Through the Looking Glass* by Lewis Carroll (1872).

Write a list of 10 things you'd like to do when you are older. Your ideas can be crazy or serious. It's up to you . . . just as long as you write them in your best joined-up handwriting. Don't forget to number your list 1 to 10.

Ten things to do challenge

Handwriting: practising all joins; numerals 1 to 10.

A comma can make a big difference.

Copy the sentence that labels the picture.

Kenji walked on, his head held high.

Kenji walked on his head, held high.

Trace then write. Then illustrate each sentence.

Let's eat Dad.

Let's eat, Dad.

Handwriting: practising all joins. **Grammar:** pronoun ('us' in Let's) **Punctuation**: comma to separate a phrase.

All was a-shake and a-shiver – glints and gleams and sparkles, rustle and swirl, chatter and bubble.

Assessment 1

Date ______________________

Rewrite the text above using all the joins you have learned.

Assessment 2

Date ______________________

Rewrite the text above using all the joins you have learned.

Grammar: adjectives; common nouns; doing verbs; saying verbs. **Literary elements:** quote from *The Wind in Willows* by Kenneth Grahame (1908).

All was a-shake and a-shiver – glints and gleams and sparkles, rustle and swirl, chatter and bubble.

Assessment 3

Date ____________________

Rewrite the text above using all the joins you have learned.

Assessment 4

Date ____________________

Rewrite the text above using all the joins you have learned.

Grammar: adjectives; common nouns; doing verbs; saying verbs. **Literary elements:** quote from *The Wind in Willows* by Kenneth Grahame (1908).

Read each of the criteria listed below. When you think you have achieved each one, write the date and sign off.

Criteria	Done	Date and sign off
My letters are the right shape.	☐	
My letters are a consistent size.	☐	
My letters are a consistent height.	☐	
My letters sit on the blue line correctly.	☐	
My letters are the same slope.	☐	
The space between my letters is regular.	☐	
The space between my words is regular.	☐	
My joins are smooth.	☐	
I can do all the joins.	☐	
My writing flows.	☐	
I can write quite quickly when I need to.	☐	
Others can easily read my joined handwriting.	☐	

Have you signed off on each of the criteria for fluent and legible handwriting? You've successfully completed your handwriting journey.

Congratulations!